Chef-A-Rella

Story by
Marie Agerton

Marie Agerton

Pictures by Lori Keehner

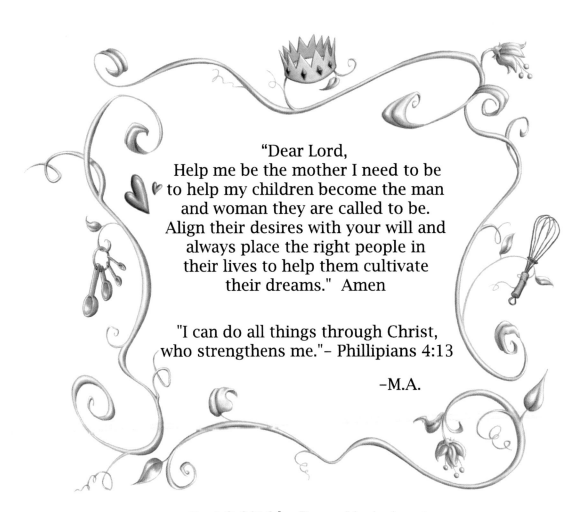

"Dear Lord,
Help me be the mother I need to be
to help my children become the man
and woman they are called to be.
Align their desires with your will and
always place the right people in
their lives to help them cultivate
their dreams." Amen

"I can do all things through Christ,
who strengthens me."– Phillipians 4:13

–M.A.

Text © 2016 by Tonya Marie Agerton

Illustrations © 2016 by Lori Keehner

Printed in the United States of America

First Printing, 2016

PB ISBN 978-1-5330-4803-5

HC ISBN 978-0-692-70194-2

Visit the illustrator's website at http://www.lorikeehner.com

visit Amazon to order additional copies.

There once lived a princess by the name of Danielle, and she loved all things cooking, and baking as well.

But her mother believed that no princess should cook. It was far, far too messy—pots covered in gook.

They become ballerinas. They DON'T learn to bake. That's what princesses do, and please make no mistake!

So when Princess Danielle was sent up to her room,
to practice ballet with her heart full of gloom,

rather than prance on the points of her toes,
she turned on the TV and she watched cooking shows.

Oh, to be a great chef on the TV one day!
She'd teach all of her viewers her famous *soufflé*.

"I don't hear any dancing!" her queen mama yelled.
"I'm rehearsing my twirl," shouted Princess Danielle.

She danced to the mirror that hung on the wall.
She took a small curtsy and did a *royale*.

"Good morning," she said in her French-est accent.
"I will be your show host in zis cooking segment.

Today we will make ze *chicken cordon bleu*.
I am Princess Danielle; Chef-A-Rella to you."

"**F**irst things first, *mes amis,*
as I always say.

So, wash up
your hands—
keep zose
germies away.

Now, get out your
chicken,

ze ham,

and some cheese.

You can even add

garnish,

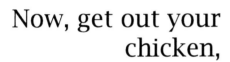

if zat's what you please."

She leaned in to her mirror. "I'll give you a tip."
Then she did a *plié* with a bend of her hip.

"Everyone thinks that my cooking is boss,
but my secret is just guaca-*mol*-e sauce!"

She pretended to nibble a dainty, small bite.
"Yum yummy! A dance in your mouth,
and it fills up the tummy!"

"Princess Danielle! I can see that you're playing.
You're standing around when you should be *plié*-ing!

Now straighten your tutu and please fix that hair!
We have guests here for dinner.

You have to be there!"

So Princess Danielle hurried straight out the door,
just glad not to practice a single step more.

"So this is Danielle? She's the whiz at ballet?"
asked the guests in the hall, to her utter dismay.

"Well, don't be so coy,
show us all what you've got.

Your mom says you're brilliant,
so give it a shot."

So she bravely attempted a fumbling leap.
She knocked down two glasses with one graceless sweep.

She spun the wrong way on her *tour-en-l'air*,

and then *pas-de-bourrée'd*
swiftly into a chair!

She stopped with a blush and a quick sideways glance.
"I'm sorry, the truth is, I don't like to dance."

The queen made it out to be all a big joke.
She laughed and gave Princess Danielle a sharp poke.

"That's crazy talk! Everyone trips now and then.
You love to dance, darling. Now, do it again!"

ut before she could start, her king daddy spoke up.
He stroked at his beard as he set down his cup.

"Why, Danielle, this is something I've never heard of.
If a princess can't dance—well then, what *does* she love?"

"What I love is to cook, King Daddy, and bake.
Lip-smacking meals are what I want to make."

Her daddy just smiled and said, "Sounds good to me!"
"Well," said Queen Mama, "I just don't agree!

A princess pays chefs to do all of the cooking.
Your job is to just be polite and good-looking."

"Speaking of chefs," said the king,
"What is taking so long?
My stomach is singing a feed-me-now song.

Princess Danielle, please go check on the food.
Being hungry puts kings in a very bad mood."

"Oh, Chef!" called Danielle. He was nowhere in sight.
There was nothing on boil, not a fire alight.

The chef was asleep on a basket of grapes,
exhausted from teaching Danielle to make crepes.

But she had an idea to get Chef off the hook.
She'd prepare the whole meal.

Now, what would she cook?

It would have to be done in a scurrying hurry.

"Et Voilà!"

said Danielle.

"I will make chicken curry!"

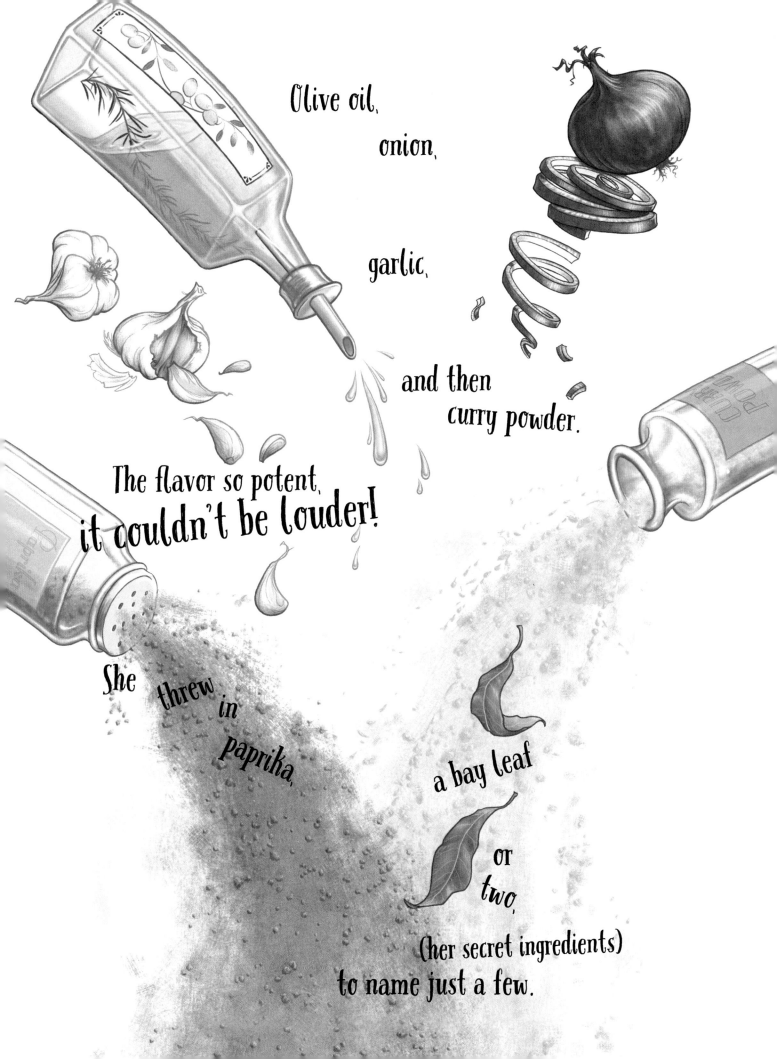

Olive oil,

onion,

garlic,

and then
curry powder.

The flavor so potent,
it couldn't be louder!

She
threw
in
paprika,

a bay leaf
or
two,

(her secret ingredients)
to name just a few.

Then she pounded the chicken, added fresh tomato paste,
and she tossed in some salt just to give it more taste.

It was Chef-A-Rella heaven, the air filled with spices,
and such joyful noise rose from the whirring devices.

With the last garnish placed, the last lemon zest curled,
she tried to wake Chef. He was dead to the world!

So, she did her best leap with a whole loaf of bread,
and then as she passed by, let it land on his head.

At last, the chef opened his bleary blue eyes.
He gasped at the food. Oh my, what a surprise!

"I won't tell," said Danielle, "if you'll just serve the meal. But you can't tell I cooked it, and that is the deal!"

So the chef bustled in and served plates off his tray,
and everyone started to eat right away.

Everyone loved it, the whole dinner crowd,
and it made Danielle happy and so very proud.

But poor Chef was ashamed to be getting the credit.
So, he took a deep breath and he came out and said it.

"I adore the applause for the food on your plates.
But, Princess Danielle cooked
the food that you ate.

The *hors d'oeuvres,*
the main meal,

and that fine
dessert number.

$\int$he did it herself while
I was deep in a slumber!"

Nobody there
could believe
their own ears.

"Well,

raise your cups,
friends.

Give my baby
some cheers!"

"It's divine," said the queen, her mouth full of entrée, "but she must have a focus, and it must be BALLET!"

"But, we can't make her dance if it's not in her heart. S'pose we hang up those slippers and order our princess her own Cuisinart!"

"Oh, Mom," said Danielle . . .

"I know that you
dream I'll be good
at ballet . . .

. . . but my dreams
are of truffles, and warm *crème
brûleé*."

"Give me a spoon
and a big oven mitten,
a kitchen to cook in,
and boy,
I'll be smitten!"

"I don't mean
to be bad,

or ignore all your wishes.
I'm just crazy for baking
and making fine dishes."

At last the queen sighed
and she smiled at her girl.

"I assumed that all
princesses wanted to twirl.

But, if cooking and baking is
what makes your heart dance . . .

. . . **W**ell, I know a great cooking school over in France.

I love you Princess Danielle,
my little **Chef-A-Rella!**"